DIVINE MERCY EXPLAINED

Keys to the Message and Devotion

by
Fr. Michael E. Gaitley, MIC

MARIAN PRESS
STOCKBRIDGE MA 01263

2015

Available from:
Marian Helpers Center
Stockbridge, MA 01263

Prayerline:1-800-804-3823
Orderline: 1-800-462-7426
Website: www.thedivinemercy.org

ISBN: 978-1-59614-272-5
First edition (4th printing): 2015
Printed in the United States of America

The main text of this work is an excerpt from
The 'One Thing' Is Three by Fr. Michael Gaitley, MIC,
which has received the following:

† IMPRIMATUR †
Timothy A. McDonnell
Bishop of Springfield, Massachusetts
November 4, 2012

IMPRIMI POTEST
Rev. Kazimierz Chwalek, MIC
Provincial Superior
October 19, 2012

NIHIL OBSTAT
Rev. Mark S. Stelzer, STD
Censor Librorum
October 17, 2012

Text from the English Edition of the *Diary of St. Maria
Faustina Kowalska: Divine Mercy in My Soul*, © 1987 Marian
Fathers of the Immaculate Conception of the B.V.M.,
Stockbridge, MA 01263.

CONTENTS

INTRODUCTION

I'm writing this booklet to help people fully discover the amazing Divine Mercy message and devotion. And I do mean *amazing*. It's been called "the greatest grassroots movement in the history of the Catholic Church"[1] and has changed millions of lives. Mine is one of them. I first learned about Divine Mercy in college, and it touched my heart so deeply that I decided to dedicate my life to spreading the word. I remember saying to myself at the time, "Why haven't I heard this before? This is incredible! People need to hear this!"

Perhaps you yourself have already experienced something of this message and devotion. For instance, maybe you've seen the Image of Divine Mercy, which is reproduced on the cover. Or maybe you've prayed the Chaplet of Divine Mercy, which has become popular in so many homes and parishes. Then again, maybe you haven't had any experience with it, and you're just curious as to what this "Divine Mercy" stuff is all about.

Whatever your exposure to the message and devotion, this booklet is for you. It's even for those who have been devoted to Divine Mercy for years. For instance, my friend Vinny Flynn, who has spent several decades in full-time Divine Mercy work, read the rough draft of this manuscript and exclaimed, "Finally! A quick, clear, and easy way to understand Divine Mercy!" Then, he encouraged me to have it published, and so, here we are.

Now, what exactly is this booklet going to do? Basically, it's going to give you a brief and easy-to-understand introduction to Divine Mercy. Specifically, you'll learn some of the history and context, all the essential elements of the devotion, and how to live the message. In short, it's everything you need to know! It's Divine Mercy *explained*. Finally, as a bonus, I've included two helpful appendices: One contains valuable prayers and the other has powerful statements about Divine Mercy from Popes John Paul II and Benedict XVI.

Alright, so let's begin. But before we cover the message and devotion, let's look at Divine Mercy in general.

DIVINE MERCY IN GENERAL

Divine Mercy gets to the heart of Sacred Scripture. In fact, as the *Catechism of the Catholic Church* says, "The Gospel is the revelation in Jesus Christ of God's mercy to sinners."[2] Right there: That summarizes it. Divine Mercy is the Gospel. It's the good news. And so, it gets to the very center of our faith. Moreover, in the words of Pope Benedict XVI, "Divine Mercy is not a secondary devotion, but an integral dimension of Christian faith and prayer."[3] Benedict even goes so far as to say, "[M]ercy is the central nucleus of the Gospel message."[4] (See Appendix Two for more Divine Mercy quotes from Popes Benedict and John Paul.)

Okay, so what is Divine Mercy? What is this thing that gets to the heart of Sacred Scripture and to the very center of our faith? To begin, mercy is "love's second name."[5] It's a particular kind of love, a particular mode of love when it encounters suffering, poverty, brokenness, and sin. *Divine* Mercy is when God's love meets us and helps us in the midst of our suffering and sin. In fact, because this side of eternity we're all sinners and because suffering is our lot in life, God's love for us here always takes the form of mercy. It's always the Lord stepping out in compassion to help us poor, weak, and broken sinners. From our perspective, then, *every good we receive* is an expression of Divine Mercy.

THE MESSAGE OF DIVINE MERCY

The *message* of Divine Mercy is something that's most associated with a Polish nun who died in 1938, about a year before the start of World War II. She's known today as St. Maria Faustina Kowalska. Now, St. Faustina was a mystic. In other words, she received extraordinary experiences of the Lord Jesus in prayer. In fact, Jesus appeared to her and even spoke with her.

Of course, Jesus didn't reveal some new Gospel when he appeared to St. Faustina. I mean, he already revealed everything he needed to say 2,000 years ago to the Apostles and through Sacred Scripture. So, why did he do it? Why did he appear to Faustina? Actually, why does he appear to *any* mystic for that matter?

God sometimes appears to mystics because he has a prophetic message for a particular time in history, and he uses particular men and women to share his message. Sometimes it's to remind us of something that's been forgotten. Sometimes it's a warning. At other times, it's a message of comfort. Or it may simply be a call to conversion. Whatever it is, it doesn't change the Bible. Rather, it brings us back to it at a certain time in history.

Okay, so what's the particular and important message that God wants to give to us in our modern time through St. Faustina? Simple. He wants to remind us of the heart of Sacred Scripture, namely, *his mercy for us sinners*. In fact, he's saying to us sinners, "Now is the time of mercy. Now is a time of *extraordinary* mercy! Now is a time when I want to give especially great graces to the human race. I want to pour out my mercy in a big way."

Why would God say this? Why would he want to give such great graces in our time? I think

St. John Paul II explained it best. First, he pointed out something we all know: namely, that there are all kinds of blessings in our contemporary society. For instance, modern technology has done so much to make life easier for us. Just think of e-mail, cell phones, smartphones, and air-conditioning. All these things are blessings. Yet, in the midst of these blessings and in some ways because of the very same advances in technology that brought them, John Paul would say that *evil has a reach and power in our day like never before*. Indeed, our time, sadly, is marked by unprecedented evil. Despite this, John Paul would also say, "Be not afraid." Why should we not be afraid? Because of what St. Paul writes in Romans, "Where sin increased, grace abounded all the more" (5:20). In other words, God is not outdone by evil. So, in a time of great evil, God wants to give even greater graces, and in our time, the graces are *huge*, precisely because there's so much sin.

Basically, then, what I want to share in the remainder of this introduction to Divine Mercy, this Divine Mercy *explained*, is how we can tap into the extraordinary graces of our time. Which makes sense, right? I mean, if there are tons of graces available to us, why not gather them in?

Alright, so how do we do it? How do we get the great graces of Divine Mercy in our time? One important way to get them is to live out a devotion to Divine Mercy, and learning how to live it out is easy. All you need to know is one, little word — actually, it's a little bird: finch. F-I-N-C-H. Finch. If you remember this word, you've got it. But now I've got to explain it. Okay, so let's get started with **F-I-N-C-H**,[6] beginning with "F."

F = Feast. What feast? The Feast of Divine Mercy, also known as Divine Mercy Sunday. Divine Mercy Sunday falls on the Second Sunday of Easter, which is my favorite day of the year. I hope that by the time I finish explaining it, it will be your favorite day also.

What's so great about Divine Mercy Sunday? Well, look at it this way: What's the most important feast day of the year? Easter, right? And how many days is Easter? We celebrate it for eight full days, which is why we call it the *Octave* of Easter. But the last day is the greatest of all. The eighth day. It's the climax of the whole feast. Well, Divine Mercy Sunday is the eighth day of Easter, the climax of the entire Easter celebration. In a sense, it's the most important day of the most important feast![7]

Now, Divine Mercy Sunday existed *way* before St. Faustina. In fact, it has its roots in the Easter celebrations of the early Church.[8] Well, when Jesus told Faustina that he wanted the feast celebrated, she asked some priests and theologians about it, and they told her, "There already is such a feast." So, Faustina went back to Jesus and told him, "They tell me that there already is such a feast, and so why should I talk about it?" Jesus responded, **"And who knows anything about this feast? No one!"**[9] In other words, the great feast of mercy had been forgotten and was almost completely unknown.

So, I imagine Jesus saying to Faustina, "Look, I want people to know and celebrate this feast. And to sweeten the deal, I promise to give great graces on Divine Mercy Sunday." Specifically, he told her:

> **On that day** [Divine Mercy Sunday], **the very depths of My tender mercy are opened. I pour out a whole ocean of graces upon those souls who approach the fount of My mercy. ... On that day, all the divine floodgates through which graces flow are opened.**[10]

When I first read about these promises of grace attached to celebrating Divine Mercy Sunday, I decided to test it out. So, when the day arrived, I prayed all day long for my dad who was in need of conversion. Well, his conversion happened that very day! And 15 years later, it has still stuck. Now, of course, it doesn't always work like that, but thousands upon thousands of people attest to the super-power of prayer offered on Divine Mercy Sunday. ... But I still haven't gotten to my favorite part of Divine Mercy Sunday, what I call "the clean slate grace."

Regarding Divine Mercy Sunday, Jesus told St. Faustina, **"The soul that will go to Confession and receive Holy Communion shall obtain complete forgiveness of sins and punishment."**[11] Now, that's a big deal. It means that if we were to die right after receiving this grace, then we wouldn't have to go to purgatory! In other words, our slate is wiped clean. In fact, the theologian who was assigned by the future Pope John Paul II to investigate the question "What is the grace of Mercy Sunday?" likened the grace to a *second baptism*.[12] Of course, it's not the same as Baptism, but it is an extraordinary grace of being cleansed of sin and the punishment due to sin.

Unfortunately, a lot of people confuse the great grace of Divine Mercy Sunday with a plenary indulgence. It's not the same thing. To get a plenary indulgence, you need to do the indulgenced act, pray for the intentions of the Holy Father, go to confession (within 20 days), receive Holy Communion, and be detached from all sin.

That last one is the kicker. Are we detached from all sin? I don't know. But I once read a story that St. Philip Neri was speaking to a large crowd of people who had gathered for some Church event to receive a plenary indulgence, and the Holy Spirit told St. Philip that only two people in the whole crowd were going to receive the plenary indulgence: Philip himself and a seven-year-old boy — presumably because everyone else was attached to sin.

Now, the good news about the grace of Divine Mercy Sunday is that to receive it, you simply need to go to confession before or on the feast — the experts say that sometime during Lent suffices — be in the state of grace (no mortal sin), and receive Holy Communion with the intention of obtaining the promised grace. Of course, we should also do acts of mercy such as forgiving people, praying for others, and having the intention to be more merciful to our neighbor.

Okay, so that explains the feast. Now let's look at the next letter, "I," as in F-I …

I = Image. What image? The Image of Divine Mercy. Jesus told St. Faustina to have an image painted just as he looked when he appeared to her. She obeyed and had it painted by a Polish artist, Eugene

Kazimirowski. It took him more than 12 tries before Faustina accepted it as satisfactory.[13]

As you can see from the image on the inside back cover, Jesus' right hand is raised in blessing. Also, he's taking a step toward us, and two rays of light issue from his Heart: a red ray and a pale ray, representing the blood and water that gushed forth from his pierced side on the Cross. At the bottom of the image, Jesus wanted a prayer to be written, "Jesus, I trust in you." He also promised to give great graces through it. For instance, one time, he said:

> **I am offering people a vessel with which they are to keep coming for graces ... that vessel is this image with the signature, "Jesus, I trust in You." By means of this image, I shall be granting many graces to souls.[14]**

I've met tons of people who have experienced special graces through the Divine Mercy image. One grace that comes through the image is this: It heals the way people often mistakenly view God. Here's what I mean. People too often have a false image of God. They're afraid of him and see him as some mean ogre just out to ruin their fun. Well, the Image of Divine Mercy helps to change that. In it, we discover our Merciful Savior who surely calls us to conversion but who also blesses us, loves us, and is deserving of all of our trust.

Next, we come to the letter "N," as in F-I-**N** …

N = Novena. What novena? The Novena to Divine Mercy. A novena is basically nine days of prayer in a row. Jesus taught St. Faustina a novena that he wanted her to pray and that we can all pray. Each day, he asked that a different group of people be entrusted to him (for example, "all sinners" on day one and "all priests and religious" on day two). You can find the text for the entire Novena in Appendix One, so I won't say more about the text here.

Before moving to the next point, I'd just like to answer a question that people often ask about the novena: "When should I begin?" Well, it can be prayed at any time,[15] but a special time to pray it is in preparation for Divine Mercy Sunday. The starting date for the novena, combined with praying the Chaplet of Divine Mercy, is Good Friday, and it ends on the Saturday after Easter Sunday, the day before Divine Mercy Sunday. (Novenas typically end the day before the feast.) While you don't have to pray this novena to obtain the grace of Divine Mercy Sunday, it is a good way to prepare, and Jesus promised, **"By this novena, I will grant every possible grace to souls."**[16]

Now we come to letter "C" as in F-I-N-C …

C = Chaplet. What chaplet? The Chaplet of Divine Mercy. This is a prayer that's prayed on ordinary rosary beads, and it's pretty popular today — perhaps because it can be prayed in a short amount of time (about seven minutes).

I think another reason why the chaplet is so popular is because it's such an incredibly powerful prayer. Why is it so powerful? Because it draws its strength from the holiest and mightiest prayer there is: the Mass. In other words, the Chaplet of Divine Mercy is a kind of extension of the prayer of the Mass. In fact, it's a kind of extension of what I call the "supercharged moment of the Mass." Here's what I mean: It's an extension of that moment when the priest at the altar takes the Body and Blood of Christ into his hands and offers it up to the Father with these words:

> Through him, and with him, and in him,
> O God, almighty Father, in the unity of
> the Holy Spirit, all glory and honor is yours
> forever and ever. Amen.

That's supercharged because, at the Mass, Jesus is giving himself Body, Blood, Soul, and Divinity into our hands: literally, in the hands of the priest and spiritually, in the hands of all the lay faithful who are uniting their own sacrifices to the offering of the priest at the altar. Together, each in his own way, we offer Jesus' infinite sacrifice of love to the Father. That's the power of the Mass. It's Jesus' own sacrifice of love in our hands, held up to the Father, and the Father can't resist such a perfect sacrifice of love. It really is the perfect prayer.

Now, the chaplet is an extension of that moment of the Mass, because on the "Our Father" beads of the rosary, we pray, "Eternal Father, I offer You the Body and Blood, Soul and Divinity of Your dearly beloved Son, our Lord Jesus Christ in atonement for our sins and those of [what? … my family? … my city? … no, not just that …] *the whole world*." So, it's a bold prayer: It's for the whole world! And it can be bold, because it relies on infinite merits: Christ's infinite sacrifice of love on the Cross. Alright, so this explains the "Our Father" beads.

On each "Hail Mary" bead, we pray, "For the sake of His sorrowful Passion, have mercy on us and on the whole world." In other words, as we're holding up to the Father his Son's infinite sacrifice of love, we keep repeating: "Mercy, mercy, mercy." More specifically, we keep praying, "Have mercy on us and on the whole world." And this is powerful. Believe me. I've seen its power. I've heard the testimonies. And you know who it's most powerful for? The dying. Our Heavenly Father said to St. Faustina,

> **When this chaplet is said by the bedside of a dying person ... unfathomable mercy envelops the soul, and the very depths of My tender mercy are moved for the sake of the sorrowful Passion of My Son.**[17]

Also, Jesus made several comforting promises to those who pray the chaplet:

> **Say unceasingly the chaplet that I have taught you. Whoever will recite it will receive great mercy at the hour of death. ... Even if there were a sinner most hardened, if he were to recite this chaplet only once, he would receive grace from My infinite mercy.**[18]

> **The souls that say this chaplet will be embraced by My mercy during their lifetime and especially at the hour of their death.**[19]

> **Oh, what great graces I will grant to souls who say this chaplet; the very depths of My tender mercy are stirred for the sake of those who say the chaplet.**[20]

My daughter, encourage souls to say the chaplet which I have given to you. It pleases Me to grant everything they ask of Me by saying the chaplet. When hardened sinners say it, I will fill their souls with peace, and the hour of their death will be a happy one. [21]

Okay, that was C for chaplet. To learn how to pray the chaplet, see Appendix One. Now, on to the last letter: "H," as in F-I-N-C-H …

H = Hour. What hour? The Hour of Great Mercy. Because Jesus died on the Cross for us at 3 p.m., every day between 3-4 in the afternoon is known as the Hour of Great Mercy. During this hour, Jesus asked St. Faustina to pray the Stations of the Cross, provided her duties permitted it. [22] But he went on to say:

If you are not able to make the Stations of the Cross, then at least step into the chapel for a moment and adore, in the Blessed Sacrament, My Heart, which is full of mercy; and should you be unable to step into the chapel, immerse yourself in prayer there where you happen to be … and if only for a brief moment, immerse

yourself in My Passion, particularly in My abandonment at the moment of agony.[23]

I love that. What Jesus wants above all, through this devotion, is that we have mercy on him![24] In other words, he wants us to recall his sacrifice of love. He wants us to think about what he did for us on the Cross. He simply wants our love. So, let's get "the three o'clock habit" and remember Jesus' sacrifice of love for us, even if only for a moment.

Oh, and one other thing about the Three O'clock Hour: Jesus promised that it's a huge time of grace: **"This is the hour of great mercy for the whole world. ... I will refuse nothing to the soul that makes a request of Me in virtue of My Passion."**[25] Thus, I look at this hour as a kind of mini-Mercy Sunday that we have *every day*. So, it's also a great time to pray for our loved ones, especially for the conversion of unrepentant sinners, and to recite the Chaplet of Divine Mercy. For a summary of the ways we can observe the Hour of Great Mercy, see this endnote.[26]

CONCLUSION

Okay, so there we go: Divine Mercy *explained*. Now you have everything you need to know about the Divine Mercy devotion and how to tap into the great graces

God offers us through it. Just remember FINCH, F-I-N-C-H, where F = Feast of Divine Mercy; I = Image of Divine Mercy; N = Novena of Divine Mercy; C = Chaplet of Divine Mercy; and H = Hour of Great Mercy.

Of course, we haven't only been covering the devotion. We've also learned some of the basics of the Divine Mercy *message*. But there's a bit more we should know regarding how to live it. Fr. George Kosicki's teaching tool, the "ABC's of Mercy," will help us.

By the way, before we begin, I should mention that living the Divine Mercy message and devotion to the full presupposes that one actively participates in the Sacraments. The Sacraments are the true sources and fountains of God's mercy.

A = Ask for mercy. In Sacred Scripture, Jesus tells us, "Ask and it will be given to you ... for everyone who asks receives" (Mt 7:7, 8). In the *Diary of St. Faustina,* Jesus reminds us of this idea:

> **Souls that make an appeal to My mercy delight Me. To such souls I grant even more graces than they ask. I cannot punish even the greatest sinner if he makes an appeal to My compassion.[27] [B]eg for mercy for the whole world.[28] No soul that has called upon My mercy has been disappointed.[29]**

B = Be merciful in deed, word, and prayer. As we learned earlier, mercy is love's second name. It's a particular kind of love, a particular mode of love when it encounters suffering, poverty, brokenness, and sin. But it's not just a movement of the heart. It's not just feeling compassion for someone. To be true, mercy must also be put into action. So, mercy is really two movements: heart and arms. The "heart" part is the movement of compassion — it's something we feel. The "arms" part is the movement to alleviate the suffering of another — it's something we do. And what should we do? Jesus tells us in the *Diary*:

> **I am giving you three ways of exercising mercy toward your neighbor: the first — by deed, the second — by word, the third — by prayer. In these three degrees is contained the fullness of mercy, and it is an unquestionable proof of love for Me. By this means a soul glorifies Me and pays reverence to My mercy.**[30]

So, mercy in action is mercy in deed, word, and prayer. And whenever our hearts are moved to compassion, wherever we are, we can always put this compassion into action either by some deed that helps alleviate another person's suffering, by some word that comforts or assists them, or by prayer.

As St. Faustina wrote: "If I cannot show mercy by deeds or words, I can always do so by prayer. My prayer reaches out even there where I cannot reach out physically."[31] Of course, one of the great prayers of mercy, as we learned earlier, is the Chaplet of Divine Mercy.

C = Completely Trust. Trust in the mercy of God gets to the heart of the message of Divine Mercy, which is why the Image of Divine Mercy has the prayer at the bottom, "Jesus, I trust in you." Now, trust does not mean that we have license to go about sinning as we please. Rather, it implies that we repent of our sins. Anyway, here are some beautiful quotes from the *Diary* that have to do with trust:

> **Encourage the souls with whom you come in contact to trust in My infinite mercy. Oh, how I love those souls who have complete confidence in Me — I will do everything for them.**[32]

> **Why are you fearful and why do you tremble when you are united to Me? I am displeased when a soul yields to vain terror. Who will dare to touch you when you are with Me? Most dear to Me is the soul that strongly believes in My goodness**

and has complete trust in Me. I heap My confidence upon it and give it all it asks.[33]

I desire that the whole world know My infinite mercy. I desire to grant unimaginable graces to those souls who trust in My mercy.[34]

I am Love and Mercy itself. When a soul approaches Me with trust, I fill it with such an abundance of graces that it cannot contain them within itself, but radiates them to other souls.[35]

Sooner would heaven and earth turn into nothingness than would My mercy not embrace a trusting soul.[36]

Alright, now that we know our ABC's of mercy and FINCH, we're all set to live the Divine Mercy message and devotion to the full. For more information on Divine Mercy, I invite you to visit www.TheDivineMercy.org. Also, if you have a smartphone, you can download the Marian's fully-loaded and free "Divine Mercy" app for Apple and Android mobile devices. For information about getting the *Diary of St. Faustina* or other Divine Mercy resources, see the information pages at the back of this booklet. Finally, to learn how you can solemnly celebrate Divine Mercy Sunday at your parish, visit www.CelebrateMercySunday.org.

Thanks for reading, and may God bless you with his mercy!

APPENDIX ONE
Divine Mercy Prayers

Contents

1. Chaplet of Divine Mercy

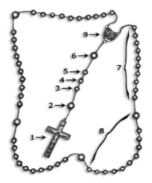

1. Make the Sign of the Cross
In the name of the Father, and of the Son, and of the Holy Spirit. Amen.

2. Optional Opening Prayers
You expired, Jesus, but the source of life gushed forth for souls, and the ocean of mercy opened up for the whole world. O Fount of Life, unfathomable Divine Mercy, envelop the whole world and empty Yourself out upon us. O Blood and Water, which gushed forth from the Heart of Jesus as a fountain of Mercy for us, I trust in You.

3. Our Father

Our Father, who art in heaven, hallowed be thy name; thy kingdom come; thy will be done on earth as it is in heaven. Give us this day our daily bread; and forgive us our trespasses, as we forgive those who trespass against us; and lead us not into temptation, but deliver us from evil. Amen.

4. Hail Mary

Hail Mary, full of grace; the Lord is with thee; blessed art thou among women, and blessed is the fruit of thy womb, Jesus. Holy Mary, Mother of God, pray for us sinners, now and at the hour of our death. Amen.

5. The Apostle's Creed

I believe in God, the Father almighty, Creator of heaven and earth, and in Jesus Christ, his only Son, our Lord, who was conceived by the Holy Spirit, born of the Virgin Mary, suffered under Pontius Pilate, was crucified, died and was buried; he descended into hell; on the third day he rose again from the dead; he ascended into heaven, and is seated at the right hand of God the Father almighty; from there he will come to judge the living and the dead. I believe in the Holy Spirit, the holy catholic Church, the communion of saints, the forgiveness of sins, the resurrection of the body, and life everlasting. Amen.

6. The Eternal Father

Eternal Father, I offer You the Body and Blood, Soul and Divinity of Your Dearly Beloved Son, Our Lord, Jesus Christ, in atonement for our sins and those of the whole world.

7. On the Ten Small Beads of Each Decade

For the sake of His sorrowful Passion, have mercy on us and on the whole world.

8. Repeat for the remaining four decades

Say the "Eternal Father" (6) on the "Our Father" bead and then 10 "For the sake of His sorrowful Passion" (7) on the following "Hail Mary" beads.

9. Conclude with Holy God (Repeat three times)

Holy God, Holy Mighty One, Holy Immortal One, have mercy on us and on the whole world.

10. Optional Closing Prayer

Eternal God, in whom mercy is endless and the treasury of compassion — inexhaustible, look kindly upon us and increase Your mercy in us, that in difficult moments we might not despair nor become despondent, but with great confidence submit ourselves to Your holy will, which is Love and Mercy itself. Amen.

2. Novena to Divine Mercy
(*Diary*, nn. 1209–1229)

(It is greatly recommended that the following novena intentions and prayers be said together with the Chaplet of Divine Mercy, since Our Lord specifically asked for a novena of chaplets, especially before the Feast of Mercy.)

First Day
Today bring to Me
ALL MANKIND, ESPECIALLY ALL SINNERS,

and immerse them in the ocean of My mercy. In this way you will console Me in the bitter grief into which the loss of souls plunges Me.

Most Merciful Jesus, whose very nature it is to have compassion on us and to forgive us, do not look upon our sins but upon our trust which we place in Your infinite goodness. Receive us all into the abode of Your Most Compassionate Heart, and never let us escape from It. We beg this of You by Your love which unites You to the Father and the Holy Spirit.

Eternal Father, turn Your merciful gaze upon all mankind and especially upon poor sinners, all enfolded in the Most Compassionate Heart of Jesus. For the sake of His sorrowful Passion show us Your mercy, that we may praise the omnipotence of Your mercy for ever and ever. Amen.

Second Day
Today bring to Me
THE SOULS OF PRIESTS AND RELIGIOUS,

and immerse them in My unfathomable mercy. It was they who gave Me strength to endure My bitter Passion. Through them as through channels My mercy flows out upon mankind.

Most Merciful Jesus, from whom comes all that is good, increase Your grace in men and women consecrated to Your service* that they may perform worthy works of mercy, and that all who see them may glorify the Father of Mercy who is in heaven.

Eternal Father, turn Your merciful gaze upon the company of chosen ones in Your vineyard — upon the souls of priests and religious; and endow them with the strength of Your blessing. For the love of the Heart of Your Son in which they are enfolded, impart to them Your power and light, that they may be able to guide others in the way of salvation and with one voice sing praise to Your boundless mercy for ages without end. Amen.

* In the original text, St. Faustina uses the pronoun "us" since she was offering this prayer as a consecrated religious sister. The wording adopted here is intended to make the prayer suitable for universal use.

Third Day
Today bring to Me
ALL DEVOUT AND FAITHFUL SOULS,

and immerse them in the ocean of My mercy. These souls brought Me consolation on the Way of the Cross. They were that drop of consolation in the midst of an ocean of bitterness.

Most Merciful Jesus, from the treasury of Your mercy, You impart Your graces in great abundance to each and all. Receive us into the abode of Your Most Compassionate Heart and never let us escape from It. We beg this grace of You by that most wondrous love for the heavenly Father with which Your Heart burns so fiercely.

Eternal Father, turn Your merciful gaze upon faithful souls, as upon the inheritance of Your Son. For the sake of His sorrowful Passion, grant them Your blessing and surround them with Your constant protection. Thus may they never fail in love or lose the treasure of the holy faith, but rather, with all the hosts of Angels and Saints, may they glorify Your boundless mercy for endless ages. Amen.

Fourth Day
Today bring to Me
THOSE WHO DO NOT BELIEVE IN GOD*
AND THOSE WHO DO NOT YET KNOW ME.

I was thinking also of them during My bitter Passion, and their future zeal comforted My Heart. Immerse them in the ocean of My mercy.

Most compassionate Jesus, You are the Light of the whole world. Receive into the abode of Your Most Compassionate Heart the souls of those who do not believe in God and of those who as yet do not know You. Let the rays of Your grace enlighten them that they, too, together with us, may extol Your wonderful mercy; and do not let them escape from the abode which is Your Most Compassionate Heart.

Eternal Father, turn Your merciful gaze upon the souls of those who do not believe in You, and of those who as yet do not know You, but who are enclosed in the Most Compassionate Heart of Jesus. Draw them to the light of the Gospel. These souls do not know what great happiness it is to love You. Grant that they, too, may extol the generosity of Your mercy for endless ages. Amen.

---

* Our Lord's original words here were "the pagans." Since the pontificate of Pope John XXIII, the Church has seen fit to replace this term with clearer and more appropriate terminology.

Fifth Day
Today bring to Me
THE SOULS OF THOSE WHO HAVE SEPARATED
THEMSELVES FROM MY CHURCH,*

and immerse them in the ocean of My mercy. During My bitter Passion they tore at My Body and Heart, that is, My Church. As they return to unity with the Church My wounds heal and in this way they alleviate My Passion.

Most Merciful Jesus, Goodness Itself, You do not refuse light to those who seek it of You. Receive into the abode of Your Most Compassionate Heart the souls of those who have separated themselves from Your Church. Draw them by Your light into the unity of the Church, and do not let them escape from the

---

* Our Lord's original words here were "heretics and schismatics," since He spoke to St. Faustina within the context of her times. As of the Second Vatican Council, Church authorities have seen fit not to use those designations in accordance with the explanation given in the Council's Decree on Ecumenism (n.3). Every pope since the Council has reaffirmed that usage. St. Faustina herself, her heart always in harmony with the mind of the Church, most certainly would have agreed. When at one time, because of the decisions of her superiors and father confessor, she was not able to execute Our Lord's inspirations and orders, she declared: "I will follow Your will insofar as You will permit me to do so through Your representative. O my Jesus, I give priority to the voice of the Church over the voice with which You speak to me" (*Diary*, 497). The Lord confirmed her action and praised her for it.

abode of Your Most Compassionate Heart; but bring it about that they, too, come to glorify the generosity of Your mercy.

Eternal Father, turn Your merciful gaze upon the souls of those who have separated themselves from Your Son's Church, who have squandered Your blessings and misused Your graces by obstinately persisting in their errors. Do not look upon their errors, but upon the love of Your own Son and upon His bitter Passion, which He underwent for their sake, since they, too, are enclosed in His Most Compassionate Heart. Bring it about that they also may glorify Your great mercy for endless ages. Amen.

Sixth Day
Today bring to Me
THE MEEK AND HUMBLE SOULS AND THE SOULS OF LITTLE CHILDREN,

and immerse them in My mercy. These souls most closely resemble My Heart. They strengthened Me during My bitter agony. I saw them as earthly Angels, who will keep vigil at My altars. I pour out upon them whole torrents of grace. Only the humble soul is capable of receiving My grace. I favor humble souls with My confidence.

Most Merciful Jesus, You Yourself have said, "Learn from Me for I am meek and humble of heart." Receive into the abode of Your Most Compassionate Heart all meek and humble souls and the souls of little children. These souls send all heaven into ecstasy and they are the heavenly Father's favorites. They are a sweet-smelling bouquet before the throne of God; God Himself takes delight in their fragrance. These souls have a permanent abode in Your Most Compassionate Heart, O Jesus, and they unceasingly sing out a hymn of love and mercy.

Eternal Father, turn Your merciful gaze upon meek souls, upon humble souls, and upon little children who are enfolded in the abode which is the Most Compassionate Heart of Jesus. These souls bear the closest resemblance to Your Son. Their fragrance rises from the earth and reaches Your very throne. Father of mercy and of all goodness, I beg You by the love You bear these souls and by the delight You take in them: Bless the whole world, that all souls together may sing out the praises of Your mercy for endless ages. Amen.

Seventh Day
Today bring to Me
THE SOULS WHO ESPECIALLY VENERATE AND GLORIFY MY MERCY,*

and immerse them in My mercy. These souls sorrowed most over my Passion and entered most deeply into My spirit. They are living images of My Compassionate Heart. These souls will shine with a special brightness in the next life. Not one of them will go into the fire of hell. I shall particularly defend each one of them at the hour of death.

Most Merciful Jesus, whose Heart is Love Itself, receive into the abode of Your Most Compassionate Heart the souls of those who particularly extol and venerate the greatness of Your mercy. These souls are mighty with the very power of God Himself. In the

* The text leads one to conclude that in the first prayer directed to Jesus, who is the Redeemer, it is "victim" souls and contemplatives that are being prayed for; those persons, that is, that voluntarily offered themselves to God for the salvation of their neighbor (see Col 1:24; 2 Cor 4:12). This explains their close union with the Savior and the extraordinary efficacy that their invisible activity has for others. In the second prayer, directed to the Father from whom comes "every worthwhile gift and every genuine benefit," we recommend the "active" souls, who promote devotion to The Divine Mercy and exercise with it all the other works that lend themselves to the spiritual and material uplifting of their brethren.

midst of all afflictions and adversities they go forward, confident of Your mercy; and united to You, O Jesus, they carry all mankind on their shoulders. These souls will not be judged severely, but Your mercy will embrace them as they depart from this life.

Eternal Father, turn Your merciful gaze upon the souls who glorify and venerate Your greatest attribute, that of Your fathomless mercy, and who are enclosed in the Most Compassionate Heart of Jesus. These souls are a living Gospel; their hands are full of deeds of mercy, and their hearts, overflowing with joy, sing a canticle of mercy to You, O Most High! I beg You O God: Show them Your mercy according to the hope and trust they have placed in You. Let there be accomplished in them the promise of Jesus, who said to them that during their life, but especially at the hour of death, the souls who will venerate this fathomless mercy of His, He, Himself, will defend as His glory. Amen.

Eighth Day
Today bring to Me
THE SOULS WHO ARE DETAINED IN PURGATORY,

and immerse them in the abyss of My mercy. Let the torrents of My Blood cool down their scorching flames. All these souls are greatly loved by Me. They are making retribution to My

justice. It is in your power to bring them relief. Draw all the indulgences from the treasury of My Church and offer them on their behalf. Oh, if you only knew the torments they suffer, you would continually offer for them the alms of the spirit and pay off their debt to My justice.

Most Merciful Jesus, You Yourself have said that You desire mercy; so I bring into the abode of Your Most Compassionate Heart the souls in Purgatory, souls who are very dear to You, and yet, who must make retribution to Your justice. May the streams of Blood and Water which gushed forth from Your Heart put out the flames of Purgatory, that there, too, the power of Your mercy may be celebrated.

Eternal Father, turn Your merciful gaze upon the souls suffering in Purgatory, who are enfolded in the Most Compassionate Heart of Jesus. I beg You, by the sorrowful Passion of Jesus Your Son, and by all the bitterness with which His most sacred Soul was flooded: Manifest Your mercy to the souls who are under Your just scrutiny. Look upon them in no other way but only through the Wounds of Jesus, Your dearly beloved Son; for we firmly believe that there is no limit to Your goodness and compassion. Amen.

Ninth Day
Today bring to Me
SOULS WHO HAVE BECOME LUKEWARM,*

and immerse them in the abyss of My mercy. These souls wound My Heart most painfully. My soul suffered the most dreadful loathing in the Garden of Olives because of lukewarm souls. They were the reason I cried out: "Father, take this cup away from Me, if it be Your will." For them the last hope of salvation is to run to My mercy.

Most compassionate Jesus, You are Compassion Itself. I bring lukewarm souls into the abode of Your Most Compassionate Heart. In this fire of Your pure love let these tepid souls, who, like corpses, filled You with such deep loathing, be once again set aflame. O Most Compassionate Jesus, exercise the omnipotence of Your mercy and draw them into the very ardor of

* To understand who are the souls designated for this day, and who in the *Diary* are called "lukewarm," but are also compared to ice and to corpses, we would do well to take note of the definition that the Savior Himself gave them when speaking to St. Faustina about on one occasion: **There are souls who thwart My efforts** (1682). **Souls without love or devotion, souls full of egoism and selfishness, proud and arrogant souls full of deceit and hypocrisy, lukewarm souls who have just enough warmth to keep themselves alive: My Heart cannot bear this. All the graces that I pour out upon them flow off them as off the face of a rock. I cannot stand them because they are neither good nor bad** (1702).

Your love, and bestow upon them the gift of holy love, for nothing is beyond Your power.

Eternal Father, turn Your merciful gaze upon lukewarm souls who are nonetheless enfolded in the Most Compassionate Heart of Jesus. Father of Mercy, I beg You by the bitter Passion of Your Son and by His three-hour agony on the Cross: Let them, too, glorify the abyss of Your mercy. Amen.

3. St. Faustina's Litany of Divine Mercy

Divine Mercy, gushing forth from the bosom of the Father,
I Trust in You.

Divine Mercy, greatest attribute of God,
I Trust in You.

Divine Mercy, incomprehensible mystery,
I Trust in You.

Divine Mercy, fountain gushing forth from the mystery of the Most Blessed Trinity,
I Trust in You.

Divine Mercy, unfathomed by any intellect, human or angelic,
I Trust in You.

Divine Mercy, from which wells forth all life and

happiness,
   I Trust in You.

Divine Mercy, better than the heavens,
   I Trust in You.

Divine Mercy, source of miracles and wonders,
   I Trust in You.

Divine Mercy, encompassing the whole universe,
   I Trust in You.

Divine Mercy, descending to earth in the Person of the Incarnate Word,
   I Trust in You.

Divine Mercy, which flowed out from the open wound of the Heart of Jesus,
   I Trust in You.

Divine Mercy, enclosed in the Heart of Jesus for us, and especially for sinners,
   I Trust in You.

Divine Mercy, unfathomed in the institution of the Sacred Host,
   I Trust in You.

Divine Mercy, in the founding of Holy Church,
   I Trust in You.

Divine Mercy, in the Sacrament of Holy Baptism,
   I Trust in You.

Divine Mercy, in our justification through Jesus Christ,
I Trust in You.

Divine Mercy, accompanying us through our whole life,
I Trust in You.

Divine Mercy, embracing us especially at the hour of death,
I Trust in You.

Divine Mercy, endowing us with immortal life,
I Trust in You.

Divine Mercy, accompanying us every moment of our life,
I Trust in You.

Divine Mercy, shielding us from the fire of hell,
I Trust in You.

Divine Mercy, in the conversion of hardened sinners,
I Trust in You.

Divine Mercy, astonishment for Angels, incomprehensible to Saints,
I Trust in You.

Divine Mercy, unfathomed in all the mysteries of God,
I Trust in You.

Divine Mercy, lifting us out of every misery,
I Trust in You.

Divine Mercy, source of our happiness and joy,
I Trust in You.

Divine Mercy, in calling us forth from nothingness to existence,
I Trust in You.

Divine Mercy, embracing all the works of His hands,
I Trust in You.

Divine Mercy, crown of all of God's handiwork,
I Trust in You.

Divine Mercy, in which we are all immersed,
I Trust in You.

Divine Mercy, sweet relief for anguished hearts,
I Trust in You.

Divine Mercy, only hope of despairing souls,
I Trust in You.

Divine Mercy, repose of hearts, peace amidst fear,
I Trust in You.

Divine Mercy, delight and ecstasy of holy souls,
I Trust in You.

Divine Mercy, inspiring hope against all hope,
I Trust in You.

Appendix Two
Divine Mercy Wisdom from the Popes

Contents

1. TOP TEN 'MERCY QUOTES' FROM POPE JOHN PAUL II

1. Right from the beginning of my ministry in St. Peter's See in Rome, I considered this message [of Divine Mercy] my special task. Providence has assigned it to me in the present situation of man, the Church and the world. It could be said that precisely this situation assigned that message to me as my task before God.

    — *Public Address at the Shrine of Merciful Love in Collevalenza, Italy on November 22, 1981.*

2. It is truly marvelous how [Sr. Faustina's] devotion to the merciful Jesus is spreading in our contemporary world and gaining so many hearts! This is doubtlessly *a sign of the times — a sign of our 20th century.* The balance of this century which is now ending, in addition to the advances which have often surpassed those of preceding eras, presents a deep restlessness and fear of the future. Where, if not in The Divine Mercy, can the world find refuge and the light of hope?

    — *Beatification Homily of Sr. Faustina, April 18, 1993.*

3. From here, in fact, went out the message of Divine Mercy that Christ himself chose to pass on to our generation through Blessed Faustina. And it is a message that is clear and understandable for

everyone. Anyone can come here, look at this picture of the Merciful Jesus, his Heart radiating grace, and hear in the depths of his own soul what Blessed Faustina heard: "Fear nothing. I am with you always" (*Diary*, q. II). And if this person responds with a sincere heart: "Jesus, I trust in you!", he will find comfort in all his anxieties and fears. In this dialogue of abandonment, there is established between man and Christ a special bond that sets love free. And "there is no fear in love, but perfect love casts out fear" (1 Jn 4:18).

— *Address to the Sisters of Our Lady of Mercy at the Shrine of the Divine Mercy in Krakow-Lagiewniki, Poland on June 7, 1997.*

4. I come here to commend the concerns of the Church and of humanity to the merciful Christ. On the threshold of the Third Millennium I come to entrust to him once more my Petrine ministry — "Jesus, I trust in you!"

The message of Divine Mercy has always been near and dear to me. [I took it] with me to the See of Peter and ... in a sense [it] forms the image of this Pontificate. ... I pray unceasingly that God will have "mercy on us and the whole world."

— *Address to the Sisters of Our Lady of Mercy at the Shrine of the Divine Mercy in Krakow-Lagiewniki, Poland, on June 7, 1997.*

5. The light of divine mercy ... will illumine the way for the men and women of the third millennium. ... Sr. Faustina's canonization has a particular eloquence: by this act, I intend today to pass this message on to the third millennium.

— *Homily of Canonization of St. Faustina, April 30, 2000.*

6. This is the happiest day of my life.

— *John Paul II's words to Dr. Valentin Fuster (the cardiologist who investigated the miraculous healing of the heart of Fr. Ron Pytel through the intercession of St. Faustina on the day of her canonization), April 30, 2000, the day the Pope also made "Divine Mercy Sunday" universally recognized by the Church.*

7. Today, therefore, in this Shrine, I wish *solemnly to entrust the world to Divine Mercy.* I do so with the burning desire that the message of God's merciful love, proclaimed here through Saint Faustina, *may be made known to all the peoples of the earth* and fill their hearts with hope. May this message radiate from this place to our beloved homeland and throughout the world. May the binding promise of the Lord Jesus be fulfilled: from here there must go forth "the spark which will prepare the world for his final coming" (cf. *Diary,* 1732). This spark needs to be lighted

by the grace of God. This fire of mercy needs to be passed on to the world. *In the mercy of God the world will find peace and mankind will find happiness!*

— *Homily at Dedication of the Shrine of Divine Mercy in Krakow-Lagiewniki on August 17, 2002.*

8. *We today have been particularly called* to proclaim this message [of Divine Mercy] before the world. We cannot neglect this mission, if God himself has called us to it through the testimony of Saint Faustina.

God has chosen our own times for this purpose. … [I]t is as if Christ, using the testimony of a lowly Sister, entered our time in order to indicate clearly the source of relief and hope found in the eternal mercy of God. *The message of merciful love needs to resound forcefully anew.* The world needs this love. The hour has come to bring Christ's message to everyone. … The hour has come when the message of Divine Mercy is able to fill hearts with hope and to become the spark of a new civilization: the civilization of love.

— *Beatification Homily of four Poles in Poland on August 18, 2002.*

9. As a gift to humanity, which sometimes seems bewildered and overwhelmed by the power of evil, selfishness and fear, the Risen Lord offers his love that pardons, reconciles and reopens hearts to love.

It is a love that converts hearts and gives peace. How much the world needs to understand and accept Divine Mercy!

Lord, who reveal the Father's love by your death and Resurrection, we believe in you and confidently repeat to you today: Jesus, I trust in you, have mercy upon us and upon the whole world.

— Regina Caeli *message for Divine Mercy Sunday, prepared by Pope John Paul II, but delivered as the Homily for the Mass for the repose of his soul on April 3, 2005.*

10. There is nothing that man needs more than Divine Mercy. ... We have a greater need than ever for a regenerating experience of mercy. ... We wish to proclaim that apart from the mercy of God there is no other source of hope for mankind. ... How greatly today's world needs God's mercy! ... How much the world needs to understand and accept Divine Mercy!

— *Compiled from various Papal Addresses from 1994–2005.*

2. Top Ten 'Mercy Quotes' from Pope Benedict XVI

1. At this time, side by side in my heart, I feel two contrasting emotions. On the one hand, a sense of inadequacy and human apprehension as I face the responsibility for the universal Church, entrusted to me yesterday as Successor of the Apostle Peter in this See of Rome. On the other, I have a lively feeling of profound gratitude to God who, as the liturgy makes us sing, never leaves his flock untended but leads it down the ages under the guidance of those whom he himself has chosen as the Vicars of his Son and has made shepherds of the flock (cf. Preface of Apostles I).

Dear friends, this deep gratitude for a gift of Divine Mercy is uppermost in my heart in spite of all. And I consider it a special grace which my Venerable Predecessor, John Paul II, has obtained for me. I seem to feel his strong hand clasping mine; I seem to see his smiling eyes and hear his words, at this moment addressed specifically to me, "Do not be afraid!"

— *First message as Pope, April 20, 2005.*

2. The Servant of God John Paul II ... wanted the Sunday after Easter to be dedicated in a special way

to Divine Mercy, and providence disposed that he should die precisely on the vigil of that day (in the hands of Divine Mercy).

The mystery of the merciful love of God was at the center of the pontificate of my venerated predecessor. Let us recall, in particular, the encyclical *Dives in Misericordia* of 1980, and the dedication of the new shrine of Divine Mercy in Krakow, in 2002.

The words he pronounced on that last occasion were as a synthesis of his magisterium, evidencing that devotion to Divine Mercy is not a secondary devotion, but an integral dimension of a Christian's faith and prayer.

— Regina Caeli *Address for Divine Mercy Sunday on April 23, 2006.*

3. On this occasion we encounter two mysteries: the mystery of human suffering and the mystery of Divine Mercy. At first sight these two mysteries seem to be opposed to one another. But when we study them more deeply in the light of faith, we find that they are placed in reciprocal harmony through the mystery of the Cross of Christ. As Pope John Paul II said in this place: "The Cross is the most profound bowing down of the Divinity towards man ... the Cross is like a touch of eternal love on the most painful wounds of humanity's earthly existence" (August 17, 2002). Dear friends who are sick, who

are marked by suffering in body or soul, you are most closely united to the Cross of Christ, and at the same time, you are the most eloquent witnesses of God's mercy. Through you and through your suffering, he bows down toward humanity with love. You who say in silence: "Jesus, I trust in you" teach us that there is no faith more profound, no hope more alive and no love more ardent than the faith, hope and love of a person who in the midst of suffering places himself securely in God's hands.

— *Address to the Sick at the Shrine of Divine Mercy in Krakow-Lagiewniki on May 27, 2006.*

4. [Being] at the Shrine of Divine Mercy in Lagiewniki allowed me to emphasize that only Divine Mercy illuminates the mystery of man. In the convent near this shrine, on contemplating the luminous wounds of the risen Christ, Sister Faustina Kowalska received a message of confidence for humanity, the message of Divine Mercy, which John Paul II echoed and of which he became the interpreter. It is a really central message for our time: Mercy as the force of God, as the divine limit against the evil of the world.

— *General Audience on May 31, 2006 following his pilgrimage to Poland where he visited the Shrine of Divine Mercy in Krakow-Lagiewniki.*

5. [A man has just been robbed and beaten, and he is lying by the side of the road. A priest and a Levite pass by on the other side of the road. Will anyone stop to help? Pope Benedict picks up the narrative here.]

And now the Samaritan enters the stage. What will he do? [Unlike the expert in the Law who had just been questioning Jesus] he does not ask how far his obligations of solidarity extend. Nor does he ask about the merits required for eternal life. Something else happens: His heart is wrenched open. The Gospel uses the word that in Hebrew had originally referred to the mother's womb and maternal care. Seeing this man in such a state is a blow that strikes him "viscerally," touching his soul. "He had compassion" — that is how we translate the text today, diminishing its original vitality. Struck in his soul by the lightning flash of mercy, he himself now becomes a neighbor, heedless of any question or danger. The burden of the question thus shifts here. The issue is no longer which other person is a neighbor to me or not. The question is about me. I have to become the neighbor, and when I do, the other person counts for me "as myself."

— *Excerpt from the book* Jesus of Nazareth, *Doubleday, 2007, p. 197.*

6. The Lord took his wounds with him to eternity. He is a wounded God; He let himself be injured through his love for us. His wounds are a sign that he understands and allows himself to be wounded out of love for us. These wounds of his: how tangible they are to us in the history of our time! Indeed, time and again, he allows himself to be wounded for our sake. What certainty of his mercy, what consolation do his wounds mean for us! … And what a duty they are for us, the duty to allow ourselves in turn to be wounded for him!

— *Homily on Divine Mercy Sunday, April 15, 2007.*

7. In our time, humanity needs a strong proclamation and witness of God's mercy. Beloved John Paul II, a great apostle of Divine Mercy, prophetically intuited this urgent pastoral need. He dedicated his second Encyclical to it and throughout his Pontificate made himself the missionary of God's love to all peoples.

After the tragic events of September 11, 2001, which darkened the dawn of the third millennium, he invited Christians and people of good will to believe that God's mercy is stronger than all evil, and that only in the Cross of Christ is the world's salvation found.

— *Angelus message on September 16, 2007.*

8. Indeed, mercy is the central nucleus of the Gospel message; it is the very name of God, the Face with which he revealed himself in the Old Covenant and fully in Jesus Christ, the incarnation of creative and redemptive Love. May this merciful love also shine on the face of the Church and show itself through the sacraments, in particular that of Reconciliation, and in works of charity, both communitarian and individual. May all that the Church says and does manifest the mercy God feels for man, and therefore for us. When the Church has to recall an unrecognized truth or a betrayed good, she always does so impelled by merciful love, so that men and women may have life and have it abundantly (cf. Jn 10:10). From Divine Mercy, which brings peace to hearts, genuine peace flows into the world, peace between different peoples, cultures and religions.

— Regina Caeli *message on Divine Mercy Sunday, March 30, 2008.*

9. God's mercy, as [Pope John Paul II] himself said, is a privileged key to the interpretation of his Pontificate. He wanted the message of God's merciful love to be made known to all and urged the faithful to witness to it (cf. Homily at Krakow-Lagiewniki, August 17, 2002). This is why he raised to the honor of the altars Sr. Faustina Kowalska, a humble Sister who, through a mysterious divine plan, became a

prophetic messenger of Divine Mercy. The Servant of God John Paul II had known and personally experienced the terrible tragedies of the 20th century and for a long time wondered what could stem the tide of evil. The answer could only be found in God's love. In fact, only Divine Mercy is able to impose limitations on evil; only the almighty love of God can defeat the tyranny of the wicked and the destructive power of selfishness and hate. For this reason, during his last visit to Poland, he said on his return to the land of his birth: "Apart from the mercy of God there is no other source of hope for mankind" (Homily at Krakow-Lagiewniki, August 17, 2002).

— *Homily on the third anniversary of the death of Pope John Paul II, April 2, 2008.*

10. Yes, dear friends, the first World Congress on Divine Mercy ended this morning with the Eucharistic Celebration in St. Peter's Basilica. I thank the organizers, especially the Vicariate of Rome, and to all the participants I address my cordial greeting which now becomes a mandate: go forth and be witnesses of God's mercy, a source of hope for every person and for the whole world. May the Risen Lord be with you always!

— Regina Caeli *message after the close of the first World Apostolic Congress on Mercy on April 6, 2008.*

3. Definitions of Mercy from Pope John Paul II

(cited from the encyclical letter, *Dives in Misericordia*)

(a) It restores to value.

[M]ercy is manifested in its true and proper aspect when it restores to value, promotes and draws good from all the forms of evil existing in the world and in man. Understood in this way, mercy constitutes the fundamental content of the messianic message of Christ and the constitutive power of His mission. His disciples and followers understood and practiced mercy in the same way. Mercy never ceased to reveal itself, in their hearts and in their actions, as an especially creative proof of the love which does not allow itself to be "conquered by evil," but overcomes "evil with good" (cf. Rom 12:21). The genuine face of mercy has to be ever revealed anew. In spite of many prejudices, mercy seems particularly necessary for our times (n. 6).

… merciful love which, by its essence, is a creative love (n. 14).

(b) It's a particular mode of love when it meets suffering.

The truth, revealed in Christ, about God the "Father of mercies," (2 Cor 1:3) enables us to "see" Him as particularly close to man especially when man is suffering, when he is under threat at the very heart of his existence and dignity (n. 2).

This love makes itself particularly noticed in contact with suffering, injustice and poverty — in contact with the whole historical "human condition," which in various ways manifests man's limitation and frailty, both physical and moral. It is precisely the mode and sphere in which love manifests itself that in biblical language is called "mercy."

... [Christ is the] incarnation of the love that is manifested with particular force with regard to the suffering, the unfortunate, and sinners, [which] makes present and thus more fully reveals the Father, who is God "rich in mercy" (n. 3).

In the preaching of the prophets, mercy signifies a special power of love, which prevails over the sin and infidelity of the chosen people (n. 4).

In the eschatological fulfillment mercy will be revealed as love, while in the temporal phase, in human history, which is at the same time the history of sin and death, love must be revealed above all as mercy and must also be actualized as mercy (n. 8).

For mercy is an indispensable dimension of love; it is as it were love's second name and, at the same time, the specific manner in which love is revealed and effected vis-a-vis the reality of the evil that is in the world, affecting and besieging man, insinuating itself even into his heart and capable of causing him to perish in Gehenna" (Mt 10:28) (n. 7).

(c) Mercy is Hesed *and* Rahamim.

In describing mercy, the books of the Old Testament use two expressions in particular, each having a different semantic nuance. First there is the term *hesed*, which indicates a profound attitude of "goodness." When this is established between two individuals, they do not just wish each other well; they are also faithful to each other by virtue of an interior commitment, and therefore also by virtue of a faithfulness to themselves. Since *hesed* also means "grace" or "love," this occurs precisely on the basis of this fidelity. The fact that the commitment in question has not only a moral character but almost a juridical one makes no difference. When in the Old Testament the word *hesed* is used of the Lord, this always occurs in connection with the covenant that God established with Israel. This covenant was, on God's part, a gift and a grace for Israel. Nevertheless, since, in harmony with the covenant entered into, God had made a commitment to respect it, *hesed* also acquired in a certain sense a legal content. The juridical commitment on God's part ceased to oblige whenever Israel broke the covenant and did not respect its conditions. But precisely at this point, *hesed*, in ceasing to be a juridical obligation, revealed its deeper aspect: it showed itself as what it was at the beginning, that is, as love that gives, love more powerful than betrayal, grace stronger than sin.

This fidelity *vis-a-vis* the unfaithful "daughter of my people"(cf. Lam 4:3, 6) is, in brief, on God's part, fidelity to Himself. This becomes obvious in the frequent recurrence together of the two terms *hesed we'e met* (= grace and fidelity), which could be considered a case of hendiadys (cf. e.g. Ex 34:6; 2 Sm 2:6; 15:20; Ps 25[24]:10; 40[39]:11-12; 85[84]:11; 138[137]:2; Mi 7:20). "It is not for your sake, O house of Israel, that I am about to act, but for the sake of my holy name" (Ez 36:22). Therefore Israel, although burdened with guilt for having broken the covenant, cannot lay claim to God's *hesed* on the basis of (legal) justice; yet it can and must go on hoping and trusting to obtain it, since the God of the covenant is really "responsible for his love." The fruits of this love are forgiveness and restoration to grace, the reestablishment of the interior covenant.

The second word which in the terminology of the Old Testament serves to define mercy is *rahamim*. This has a different nuance from that of *hesed*. While *hesed* highlights the marks of fidelity to self and of "responsibility for one's own love" (which are in a certain sense masculine characteristics), *rahamim*, in its very root, denotes the love of a mother (*rehem* = mother's womb). From the deep and original bond

— indeed the unity — that links a mother to her child there springs a particular relationship to the child, a particular love. Of this love one can say that it is completely gratuitous, not merited, and that in this aspect it constitutes an interior necessity: an exigency of the heart. It is, as it were, a "feminine" variation of the masculine fidelity to self expressed by *hesed*. Against this psychological background, *rahamim* generates a whole range of feelings, including goodness and tenderness, patience and understanding, that is, readiness to forgive.

The Old Testament attributes to the Lord precisely these characteristics when it uses the term *rahamim* in speaking of Him. We read in Isaiah: "Can a woman forget her suckling child, that she should have no compassion on the son of her womb? Even these may forget, yet I will not forget you" (Is 49:15). This love, faithful and invincible thanks to the mysterious power of motherhood, is expressed in the Old Testament texts in various ways: as salvation from dangers, especially from enemies; also as forgiveness of sins — of individuals and also of the whole of Israel; and finally in readiness to fulfill the (eschatological) promise and hope, in spite of human infidelity, as we read in Hosea: "I will heal their faithlessness, I will love them freely" (Hos 14:5) (endnote n. 52).

ENDNOTES

1 Statement of Fr. Seraphim Michalenko, MIC, world-renowned expert on the Divine Mercy message and devotion and vice-postulator for the canonization cause of Sr. Maria Faustina Kowalska.

2 *Catechism*, n. 1849.

3 Benedict XVI, *Regina Caeli* Address, Divine Mercy Sunday, April 23, 2006.

4 Ibid., Divine Mercy Sunday, March 30, 2008.

5 *Dives in Misericordia*, n. 7.

6 I'm grateful to Fr. Dan Cambra, MIC, for sharing this acronym with me.

7 See next note.

8 Divine Mercy Sunday has its roots in the Octave Day of Easter, which was celebrated in the early Church. The great theologian Gregory of Nazianzen even taught a rather bold concept that the Easter Octave Day is the "New Sunday." He distinguished the Pasch or Easter from its octave, affirming "that Sunday [meaning Easter Day] was the day of salvation, but this Sunday [meaning the Octave of Easter] is the birthday of salvation." This early Church theologian considered the Octave Day of Easter to be "more sublime" and "more wonderful" without in any way depreciating Easter Sunday itself.

It's no wonder, then, that St. Augustine in his sermons calls the whole Octave of Easter "days of mercy and pardon" and the Octave Day itself "the compendium of the days of mercy." In his *Summa Theologiae*, St. Thomas Aquinas echoes the early Fathers when he describes the Octave Day as the goal and the second perfection of Easter. For a penetrating analysis of this topic, see "A Contribution to the Discussion on the Feast of The Divine Mercy" by Fr.

Seraphim Michalenko, MIC, in *Divine Mercy: The Heart of the Gospel* (Stockbridge: Marian Press, 1999), p. 117-133.

9 *Diary*, n. 341.

10 Ibid., n. 699.

11 Ibid., n. 699.

12 See the judgment of the theologian censor on the writings attributed to the Servant of God, Faustina Kowalska in *Sacra Congregatio Pro Causis Sanctorum P.n. 1123 Cracovien. Beatificationis et canonizationis servae dei Faustinae Kowalska Instituti Sororum B.M.V.A. Misericordia (1905-1938)*, pp. 429-430.

13 That original image now hangs in the Holy Spirit Church in Vilnius, Lithuania. This image is also reproduced on the cover and inside back cover. An interesting fact about this particular image is that if you superimpose it over the Shroud of Turin, it makes nearly a perfect match!

14 *Diary*, nn. 327, 742.

15 At the National Shrine of The Divine Mercy in Stockbridge, Mass., we pray a perpetual Novena to Divine Mercy. In other words, we continually pray the days of the novena such that, after completing the ninth day, we start all over again with the first day. Our custom at the Shrine is to do this before we begin the Chaplet of Divine Mercy.

16 Ibid., n. 796. The text of the Novena to Divine Mercy can be found on pages 29-40 of this booklet.

17 Ibid., n. 811.

18 Ibid., n. 687.

19 Ibid., n. 754.

20 Ibid., n. 848.

21 Ibid., n. 1541.

22 Ibid., n. 1572.

23 Ibid., nn., 1572, 1320. Notice in this passage that Jesus especially wants us to pray the Stations of the Cross during the Hour of Great Mercy, provided that our duties permit

it. It's fitting, therefore, that the Marian Fathers of the Immaculate Conception at the National Shrine of the Divine Mercy have installed life-sized Stations of the Cross. To learn more about these beautiful bronze stations, visit: www.thedivinemercy.org/stations

24 Can we really have mercy on Jesus? In a remarkable passage from *Dives in Misericordia*, Pope John Paul II teaches that we not only can have mercy on him but should do so:

> The events of Good Friday and, even before that, in prayer in Gethsemane, introduce a fundamental change into the whole course of the revelation of love and mercy in the messianic mission of Christ. The one who "went about doing good and healing" and "curing every sickness and disease" now Himself seems to merit the greatest mercy and to *appeal for mercy*, when He is arrested, abused, condemned, scourged, crowned with thorns, when He is nailed to the cross and dies amidst agonizing torments. It is then that He particularly deserves mercy from the people to whom He has done good, and He does not receive it ...
>
> [T]he cross will remain the point of reference for other words too of the Revelation of John: "Behold, I stand at the door and knock; if anyone hears my voice and opens the door, I will come in and eat with him and he with me." In a special way, God also reveals His mercy when He invites man to have "mercy" on His only Son, the crucified one.
>
> ... Christ, precisely as the crucified one, is the Word that does not pass away, and He is the one who stands at the door and knocks at the heart of every man, without restricting his freedom, but instead seeking to draw from this very freedom

love, which is not only an act of solidarity with the suffering Son of man, but also a kind of "mercy" shown by each one of us to the Son of the eternal Father. In the whole of this messianic program of Christ, in the whole revelation of mercy through the cross, could man's dignity be more highly respected and ennobled, for, in obtaining mercy, He is in a sense the one who at the same time "shows mercy"? (nn. 7-8).

25 *Diary*, n. 1320.
26 Three Ways to Keep the Three O'clock Hour: (Based on *Diary*, nn. 1320, 1570.)

1. We can *immerse ourselves in the Lord's Passion, especially in his abandonment on the Cross*. We can do this briefly (even "for an instant") or for a longer period of time. For example, we can simply look at a crucifix, think of Jesus in his Passion, or pray the Three O'clock Prayer:

You expired, Jesus, but the source of life gushed forth for souls, and the ocean of mercy opened up for the whole world. O Fount of Life, unfathomable Divine Mercy, envelop the whole world and empty Yourself out upon us (n. 84). ... O Blood and Water, which gushed forth from the Heart of Jesus as a fount of mercy for us, I trust in You (n. 1319).

If we have more time, we can pray the sorrowful mysteries of the Rosary or make the Stations of the Cross.

2. We can *present our petitions to the Father by virtue of his Son's Passion.* Our petitions should be made with bold confidence because of the indescribable power of Jesus' Passion and the great promises attached to the Hour of Great Mercy. I recommend presenting one's petitions in the context of praying the Divine Mercy Chaplet. (Don't forget to pray for unrepentant sinners and the dying, especially for unrepentant sinners who are dying.)

3. The three o'clock hour is a great time to *visit Jesus, truly present in the Blessed Sacrament.*

[27] *Diary*, n. 1146.
[28] Ibid., n. 570.
[29] Ibid., n. 1541.
[30] Ibid., n. 742.
[31] Ibid., n. 163.
[32] Ibid., n. 294.
[33] Ibid., n. 453.
[34] Ibid., n. 687.
[35] Ibid., n. 1074.
[36] Ibid., n. 1777.

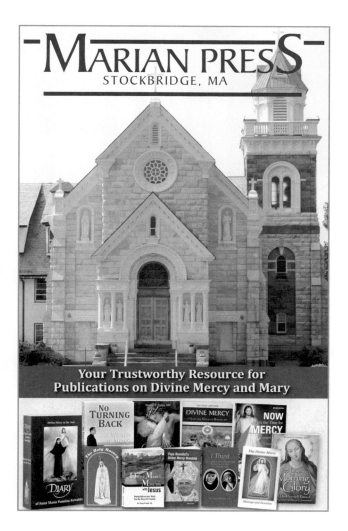

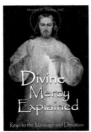

OTHER TITLES BY FR. MICHAEL GAITLEY, MIC

33 Days to Morning Glory

Begin an extraordinary 33-day journey to Marian consecration with four spiritual giants: St. Louis de Montfort, St. Maximilian Kolbe, Blessed Mother Teresa of Calcutta, and St. John Paul II. This user-friendly, do-it-yourself retreat* will bless even the busiest of people. (208 pages.)

Y10-33DAY

Consoling the Heart of Jesus

This do-it-yourself retreat* combines the *Spiritual Exercises of St. Ignatius* with the teachings of Saints Thérèse of Lisieux, Faustina Kowalska, and Louis de Montfort. (428 pages.) Includes bonus material in appendices.

Consoling the Heart of Jesus Prayer Companion
Contains the essence of Consoling spirituality and all the main prayers from the popular "do-it-yourself" retreat. (126 pages.)

Y10-CHJ

Y10-PCCHJ

The 'One Thing' Is Three*

With humor and ease, Fr. Michael Gaitley, MIC, deftly unlocks the 'one thing,' the key to the Church's wisdom, and the greatest mystery of the Catholic faith: the Most Holy Trinity. Far from being an academic read, *The 'One Thing' Is Three* makes deep theology accessible to everyday Catholics. What's more, it makes even what's familiar or forgotten new, exciting, and relevant. (400 pages.)

Y10-ONE

*Also available as a group retreat!
Visit AllHeartsAfire.org.